ENGINEERING IN ACTION

MATERIALS ENGINEERING
AND Exploring Properties

Crabtree Publishing Company
www.crabtreebooks.com

Robert Snedden

Crabtree Publishing Company

www.crabtreebooks.com

Author: Robert Snedden

Publishing plan research and development: Reagan Miller

Photo research: James Nixon

Editors: Paul Humphrey, James Nixon, Kathy Middleton

Consultant: Carolyn De Cristofano, M.Ed. STEM consultant, Professional Development Director of Engineering is Elementary (2005-2008)

Proofreader: Wendy Scavuzzo

Layout: sprout.uk.com

Cover design and logo: Margaret Amy Salter

Production coordinator and prepress technician: Margaret Amy Salter

Print coordinator: Margaret Amy Salter

Written and produced for Crabtree Publishing Company by Discovery Books

Thanks to Blue Heron STEM Education, Inc. for providing the design challenge on pages 26–27.

Photographs:
Alamy: pp. 4 (imageBROKER), 5 (DOE Photo), 6 (Gianni Muratore), 8 (www.BibleLandPictures.com), 9 top (Nature Picture Library), 19 (Susannah Ireland), 20 (Aurora Photos), 21 (Cal Sport Media), 23 top (age footstock), 23 bottom (dpa picture alliance archive).
Bigstock: pp. 9 bottom (Paha_L), 10 (mezzotint), 12 top (alabony), 12 bottom (Whiskybottle), 18 (Goodluz), 24 (Nataliya Hora), 26 (IKuvshinov).
Florida International Univeristy: p. 14 (College of Engineering and Computing).
Getty Images: pp. 25 (Kathryn Scott Osler/The Denver Post), 28 (PHILIPPE DESMAZES/AFP).
NASA: p. 29 (BYU).
Kingston University London: p. 22 (Jonathan Nixon).
Shutterstock: Cover left (Beto Chagas), middle right (Alexandre Rotenberg), bottom right (Victor Voicu), background (Marioner), top right (ArtMari)
University of Massachusetts Amherst: p. 13 top and bottom (The College of Natural Sciences).
U.S. Army: p. 15.
Wikimedia: pp. 11 top (PD-USGOV-NASA), 11 bottom (NASA/Drew Noel), 16 top (Chemical Heritage Foundation), 16 bottom (Marie-Lan Nguyen), 17 (Lisa Gansky).

Library and Archives Canada Cataloguing in Publication

Snedden, Robert, author
    Materials engineering and exploring properties / Robert Snedden.

(Engineering in action)
Includes index.
Issued in print and electronic formats.
ISBN 978-0-7787-7514-0 (bound).--
ISBN 978-0-7787-7535-5 (paperback).--
ISBN 978-1-4271-9999-7 (pdf).--
ISBN 978-1-4271-9995-9 (html)

    1. Materials--Juvenile literature. I. Title. II. Series:
Engineering in action (St. Catharines, Ont.)

TA403.2.S64 2015   j620.1'1   C2015-903438-8
                                                        C2015-903439-6

Library of Congress Cataloging-in-Publication Data

Snedden, Robert, author.
    Materials engineering and exploring properties / Robert Snedden.
        pages cm. -- (Engineering in action)
    Includes index.
    ISBN 978-0-7787-7514-0 (reinforced library binding) --
    ISBN 978-0-7787-7535-5 (pbk.) --
    ISBN 978-1-4271-9999-7 (electronic pdf) --
    ISBN 978-1-4271-9995-9 (electronic html)
    1. Materials--Properties--Juvenile literature. 2. Materials science-
-Juvenile literature. 3. Engineering--Juvenile literature. I. Title. II.
Series: Engineering in action.

    TA403.2.S63 2016
    620.1'1--dc23
                                            2015021359

Crabtree Publishing Company
www.crabtreebooks.com   1-800-387-7650

Printed in Canada/082015/BF20150630

Published in Canada
Crabtree Publishing
616 Welland Ave.
St. Catharines, ON
L2M 5V6

Published in the United States
Crabtree Publishing
PMB 59051
350 Fifth Avenue, 59th Floor
New York, New York 10118

Published in the United Kingdom
Crabtree Publishing
Maritime House
Basin Road North, Hove
BN41 1WR

Published in Australia
Crabtree Publishing
3 Charles Street
Coburg North
VIC, 3058

CONTENTS

A WORLD OF MATERIALS

We can see the work of materials engineers all around us. Many industries rely on the expertise of materials engineers. **Civil engineers** couldn't design buildings, aviation engineers couldn't build aircraft, and electronics engineers couldn't make smartphones, if it weren't for materials engineers designing and testing the materials that go into each and every product.

Making things

Every object we use is made of at least one material. That's what a material is: something from which a thing can be made. Materials in their natural state, from which useful products are made, are called **raw materials**. Some raw materials just have to be shaped to make them useful, such as stone for a building and wood to make furniture. But most materials have had to be altered in some way. Metals, plastics, and fabrics are all materials that have been processed from raw materials. Metals are extracted from rock **ores**, plastics are made from **chemicals** found in petroleum, and fabrics have to be woven from natural and human-made materials.

Strength is an important characteristic of the materials we choose for building.

Engineering the future:

Engineers are always looking for ways to improve materials. Better materials make new technologies possible. One of the most exciting things about materials engineering today is our growing ability to understand how materials are put together, right down to the invisible level of **atoms**. Materials scientists and engineers are focusing their efforts on changing the **properties** of materials by controlling their structure. With this knowledge, materials engineers hope to design new materials suited to perform any task.

Materials engineering researchers are always experimenting with new materials.

Making the right choice

So how do engineers know which materials are best for each job? First, they have to understand the properties of each material—the qualities each one has—that make it suitable for a particular use. Materials and their properties affect every aspect of the things we use. For example, they affect cost, reliability, and how environmentally friendly they are.

Engineers generally follow an eight-step process when they are trying to design a solution to a problem. Like all engineers, materials engineers may not follow this process exactly, but it generally guides their work.

Steps in the design process

Define the problem

↓

Identify criteria and constraints

↓

Brainstorm ideas

↓

Select a solution

↓

Build a model

Improve the design ← **Test the model**

↓

Communicate the solution

MATTER AND MATERIALS

All of the materials we make use of, and in fact everything around us, is made of **matter**. The air we breathe, the food we eat, the clothes we wear, the ground we walk on, and we ourselves, are all made of matter.

Matter is made up of tiny particles called atoms. There are 94 different kinds of atom that exist in nature and more have been created in the laboratory. A substance that is made up of just one kind of atom is called an **element**.

Molecules and compounds: Elements can join together in different ways to form larger particles called **molecules**. A molecule made of two or more different elements is called a compound. Most of the materials we come across in everyday life are made up of compounds. The elements can be combined to make an immense variety of compounds, each with different properties and uses.

Compounds are formed by **chemical reactions**. Newly formed compounds can have quite different properties from the original chemicals that reacted together. The chemical properties of a material tell you how it will behave when you do different things to it. They also tell you how it will react with other elements or compounds, and what new materials can be made from it. All of this is important knowledge for the materials engineer.

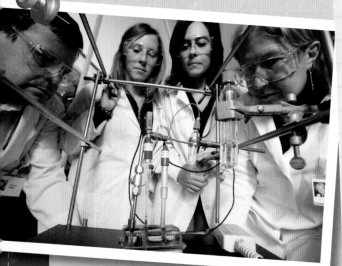

Learning about chemistry is an important part of a materials engineer's training.

THE PERIODIC TABLE

All chemicals have different properties and it is important that engineers understand them. The periodic table of the elements, devised by Dmitri Mendeleev in 1864, identifies and organizes the chemical elements by their properties. In 2006, materials engineers voted the periodic table as the "most indispensable reference tool" for materials scientists and engineers.

| | | | | | | | | | | | | | | | | | H 1 | | | | | | | | | | | | | | | | | He 2 |

Li 3	Be 4											B 5	C 6	N 7	O 8	F 9	Ne 10
Na 11	Mg 12											Al 13	Si 14	P 15	S 16	Cl 17	Ar 18
K 19	Ca 20	Sc 21	Ti 22	V 23	Cr 24	Mn 25	Fe 26	Co 27	Ni 28	Cu 29	Zn 30	Ga 31	Ge 32	As 33	Se 34	Br 35	Kr 36
Rb 37	Sr 38	Y 39	Zr 40	Nb 41	Mo 42	Tc 43	Ru 44	Rh 45	Pd 46	Ag 47	Cd 48	In 49	Sn 50	Sb 51	Te 52	I 53	Xe 54
Cs 55	Ba 56	57-71	Hf 72	Ta 73	W 74	Re 75	Os 76	Ir 77	Pt 78	Au 79	Hg 80	Tl 81	Pb 82	Bi 83	Po 84	At 85	Rn 86
Fr 87	Ra 88	89-103	Rf 104	Db 105	Sg 106	Bh 107	Hs 108	Mt 109	Ds 110	Rg 111							

La 57	Ce 58	Pr 59	Nd 60	Pm 61	Sm 62	Eu 63	Gd 64	Tb 65	Dy 66	Ho 67	Er 68	Tm 69	Yb 70	Lu 71
Ac 89	Th 90	Pa 91	U 92	Np 93	Pu 94	Am 95	Cm 96	Bk 97	Cf 98	Es 99	Fm 100	Md 101	No 102	Lr 103

In the periodic table, the elements are arranged into groups depending on their properties and atomic structure.

Physical properties

As well as understanding how materials behave chemically, materials engineers also have to be aware of how they can change physically. For example, they need to know how a material will react to changes in temperature. How much will it expand when heated? Is it **soluble** in water and likely to dissolve if it gets wet? Is it brittle and likely to break easily, like glass? Could it become brittle if it gets too cold? If materials engineers get things wrong, it can sometimes have tragic consequences. For example, the space shuttle *Challenger* and its crew were lost in 1986 because seals on the rocket boosters failed to work properly at low temperatures.

Thankfully, almost all of the space shuttle missions were safe and successful.

THE ANCIENT ART OF MATERIALS ENGINEERING

Materials engineers today make use of knowledge and experience that has been gained across thousands of years of human history.

Humans have always made inventive use of the materials around them. Many thousands of years ago, we discovered that chipping away part of a flint stone gave it a sharp edge that could be used to cut the skin and bone from dead animals. This was one of the first steps toward materials engineering.

Learning how to use metals was one of the most important human discoveries. This iron dagger and sheath date back to 1500 BCE.

Ceramics: More than 20,000 years ago, people began to discover how to change the properties of materials. Around this time, the earliest **ceramics** were first made. Ceramics are made from baked clay. The process is fairly simple. The clay is mixed with water to soften it, then shaped into an object. It is then "fired" by exposing it to high heat. This makes the clay hard. The earliest clay pots were probably hardened simply by the heat of the Sun, but early human **innovators** found they could get better results by baking their ceramics in specially made ovens called kilns.

Today, ceramics are an essential part of our world. Ceramic **insulators** keep our electricity supply safe. The electrical components in televisions and computers are made from ceramics. Ceramics are also used in hip replacements, heat shielding for spacecraft, and the tough shells for deep-ocean **submersibles**.

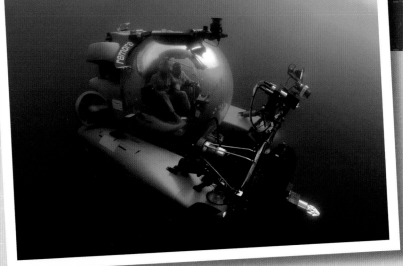

Deep-ocean submersibles rely on the strength of modern ceramics to protect them from the crushing weight of the water above them.

Metals: Some of the most important materials we use are metals. The history of their use goes back perhaps as far as 10,000 years, when the ancient Mesopotamians dug copper out of the ground and beat it into tools and ornaments. Today, iron and aluminum are two of the most commonly used metals. The ancient Egyptians were the first people to **smelt** iron around 3500 BCE, heating rocks to high temperatures to extract small amounts of the metal from them.

Aluminum today has many uses and applications in engineering. But 200 years ago, no one had ever seen any! Aluminum is never found in a pure state in nature, and it was only in the last 130 years or so that chemists and materials engineers figured out how to extract it cheaply from rock.

Worldwide, about 110 million tons (99.7 million metric tons) of aluminum is produced each year.

MAKING THE RIGHT CHOICE

It is important to choose the best materials for the job. As we have seen, that means understanding the properties and characteristics of different materials. Materials engineers often find they have to combine different materials to get the combination of properties they need for the task.

For this rider, the right choice of materials is important, not just for the bike, but for his artificial limb, too.

The materials used in a bicycle have to be strong enough to support the rider's weight, but lightweight enough that the bike can be ridden fairly easily. The bike also has to be comfortable to ride, cushioning the bumps of uneven surfaces. A glass bicycle might look wonderful, but it wouldn't be very practical!

Composites: A single material is unlikely to have all the properties necessary for a particular job. For example, the frame of a bike might be made of a **composite material**, consisting of materials such as **carbon fibers**, **resin**, metals, and ceramics. These composite frames have the advantage of being lightweight and strong but the disadvantage of being made of very expensive materials. Materials engineers always have to balance advantages and disadvantages such as these when choosing the best material for a particular job.

DR. BONNIE DUNBAR

As a veteran of five space flights, between 1985 and 1998, NASA mission specialist Dr. Bonnie Dunbar spent more than 50 days in space. Before becoming an astronaut, she was a senior research engineer with Rockwell International Space Division. She helped develop the materials used to protect the space shuttle from burning up when it reentered Earth's atmosphere. In a very real way, Dr. Dunbar was relying on her own engineering skills to get home safely.

MIRRORS IN SPACE

The James Webb Space Telescope is scheduled for launch in 2018. The engineers had to decide on a suitable material for its mirrors. They chose the metal beryllium because it had the properties they were looking for. It would keep its shape when exposed to the extreme temperatures of deep space, it is strong and lightweight, and it is not magnetic and will not interfere with the telescope's instruments. A disadvantage of working with beryllium is that its dust can be dangerous to health, so care has to be taken when using it.

NASA engineers wear special, protective suits while working on one of the mirrors of the James Webb Space Telescope.

INSPIRED BY NATURE

The very first materials humans used came from nature, such as stone and wood, and materials engineers still turn to the natural world for ideas and inspiration today. For example, the Swiss inventor Georges de Mestral came up with the idea for Velcro when he wondered how the seeds of the burdock plant attached themselves so well to his dog's coat when they were out walking.

The slippery inside of the pitcher plant inspired the development of a brand new material.

*Recently engineers discovered that the teeth of **limpets** were formed from the strongest biological material yet known, and are now looking for ways to put this to practical use.*

SLIPS

Any unfortunate insect landing on the walls inside a pitcher plant will soon find itself slipping down to its doom into a pool of digestive juices at the bottom of the plant. The plants have an unusual surface that holds in a layer of water. This acts as a **lubricant**, repelling oils found on insects' feet and causing them to slide helplessly down. Materials engineers at Harvard University in Massachusetts have found a way to mimic the pitcher plant and create a new material.

The material developed by Joanna Aizenberg and her team is called SLIPS, which stands for slippery liquid-infused **porous** surfaces. It is made of a network of microscopic fibers that hold a fluid that repels water and oil. Like the plant, it's the layer of fluid that makes SLIPS so slippery.

SLIPS could be used for many things. For example, the slippery coating could help prevent contamination of medical instruments, allow liquids to flow more smoothly through pipelines, and keep the hulls of ships clean.

Superadhesives: The gecko is a type of lizard that has a remarkable ability to cling to just about any surface. Scientists and engineers around the world have been trying to find ways to mimic the gecko's astonishing stickiness. A gecko's toes are covered with millions of tiny hairs that stick to surfaces. In 2008, engineers at the University of California in Berkeley managed to squeeze 42 million fine, but hard plastic fibers, each a hundredth the thickness of a human hair, on to 0.15 square inches (1 square centimeter) of material. The material sticks firmly if any attempt is made to slide it along a surface, but lifts off easily and leaves no residue.

The gecko's toes are one of the most remarkable things in nature.

In 2014, researchers at the University of Massachusetts developed Geckskin—an adhesive, or sticky, material that can hold over 660 lbs (300 kg) in weight. Geckskin doesn't try to directly copy the gecko's toes. Instead, it relies on something called draping adhesion which means that the Geckskin shapes itself into all of the tiny imperfections in the surface. It can be made from everyday materials such as cotton, nylon, and the sort of sealant used in bathrooms. The team said it's not about making a new material, but about making old materials perform in new ways.

Some of the team who developed Geckskin.

BECOMING A MATERIALS ENGINEER

There are many ways to become a materials engineer. Most universities now offer dedicated materials engineering courses, but many engineers have come to it from other fields. A knowledge of chemistry is essential. One way into materials engineering is through a degree in chemistry. Metallurgy—the study of metals and their properties—or another engineering discipline, such as mechanical engineering or chemical engineering, are possible ways into the field of materials engineering.

In common with other engineers, the materials engineer will be well organized, a good communicator, a team player, a problem solver, and a researcher. A materials engineer might work alongside other engineers to improve existing products or to develop something entirely new. Since everything we make involves materials, the materials engineer could work in any industry, from aerospace and computers, to construction and sports equipment. A materials engineer will probably choose to specialize in one particular type of material, such as ceramics, plastics, or metals.

Materials engineers work in research and development laboratories to develop, process, and test materials used to create a range of products.

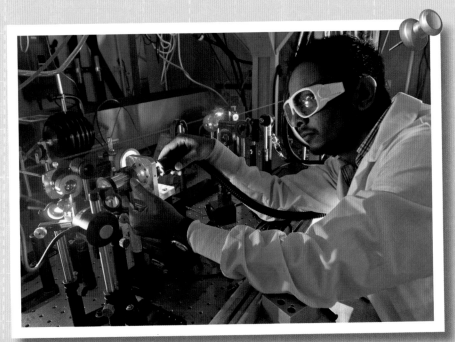

I AM A MATERIALS ENGINEER

Lee Ann Schwope is a materials engineer with Excera, a company in the United States that makes composite materials such as armor for the army, air force, and navy. One of the things she finds exciting is working with a new material called Onnex—a ceramic-metal composite, which could be used for products such as body armor, containers for molten metals, and vehicle braking systems. She knows that a lot of new materials are engineered, but only a small fraction will be useful. When she first transferred to another college, she wanted to be a chemical engineer and didn't even know materials engineering existed. She came "to love the idea that you can actually change materials by modifying the composition and therefore make it more suitable for specific applications." Schwope knows that problem-solving skills are particularly important for engineers. She feels that discovering new technologies is important, but that it is equally important to figure out how to make the technology useful to the world we live in.

Cutting-edge technology

One of the best things about being a materials engineer is that you could find yourself working right on the cutting edge of new technologies. Many materials engineers find work in research laboratories, developing new materials in areas such as medical devices (e.g., replacement heart valves) and computer technology, or investigating ways of using existing materials in better and more effective ways.

Research into new, more effective, body armor for troops is an ongoing effort.

THE PROBLEM-SOLVING PROCESS

Materials engineers are really just as much scientists as they are engineers. They are both knowledge seekers and problem solvers. They not only help make the latest scientific discoveries about the properties of materials, but also help to find ways to use these discoveries in real-world situations. Materials engineers experiment with new compounds and materials the way scientists do, but the materials engineer does this with the aim of finding the best material for a particular job.

STEPHANIE KWOLEK

Pennsylvania-born scientist and inventor Stephanie Kwolek (1923-2014) was one of the first female research chemists. She was asked to investigate fibers that were capable of performing in extreme conditions. Her experiments led to the discovery of a specialized type of plastic that had exceptional strength and stiffness. This in turn led to the invention of Kevlar, a **synthetic** material that is five times as strong as steel. Kevlar is mainly used in bulletproof vests, which have saved the lives of countless soldiers and law enforcement officers. Kevlar is also used in dozens of other products, including camping and hiking gear, and bicycle helmets.

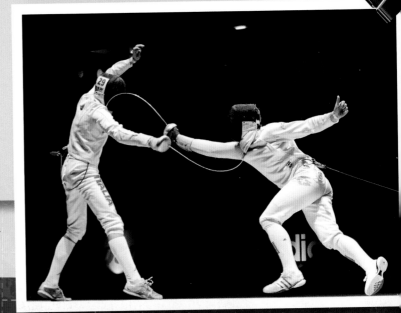

Kevlar in their suits helps protect these fencers from harm.

Identify the problem: Materials engineers work closely with other engineers and scientists to help them solve problems that involve choosing and designing the right materials for a job. It is important that everyone agrees on what they are trying to achieve, so the first step is to define the problem to be solved. For example, which would be the best materials to use if you want to design a faster, more energy-efficient computer component, or what sort of material would make the best lightweight body armor for soldiers?

Criteria and constraints: Every problem has criteria, or objectives the solution must meet, and constraints, or things that limit the possible solution. The challenge might be to design a material for use in a hockey goaltender's equipment. The criteria it must meet are that it be lightweight, doesn't restrict the goalie's movement, and gives excellent protection. At the same time, the design team will have to take a number of constraints into consideration as they search for possible solutions to the engineering problem. These might include how the materials react to cold temperatures, the cost of the materials, and whether one or more different materials will have to be used and how they will work together.

A goaltender's armor has to be lightweight so he or she can move quickly.

A QUESTION OF BALANCE

A brainstorming session is a good way to come up with a number of possible solutions to a problem.

Balancing the criteria to be met with the constraints on the project is the key to the engineering problem-solving process. Engineers will be aware that there may not be an ideal solution. When designing the material for a goalie's equipment, for example, they may have to **trade off** between strength and weight since the strongest material may be too heavy for a goaltender to wear comfortably.

Brainstorming: With the criteria and constraints firmly in mind, the project engineers will get together and start brainstorming solutions. The idea of brainstorming is to generate as many ideas as possible for solving the problem. The greater the number of ideas, the greater the chance that one of them will produce an effective solution. In a brainstorming session, there is no such thing as a bad idea. Even the craziest, most impractical suggestion might trigger an idea that leads to a workable solution.

The engineers might make use of a **concept map**, to keep track of all the ideas and their advantages and disadvantages. Armed with all of the ideas that have emerged from the brainstorming session, the engineers will then begin evaluating them, to decide which one appears to best fit the criteria and constraints of the project.

BEST PROTECTION

Combat troops may be called on to travel long distances over rough terrain. It is important to keep the weight of their gear to a minimum. Dr. Shawn Walsh of the U.S. Army Research Laboratory says soldiers always say, "can you make it lighter?" Researchers and engineers are looking at ways of using composites and ceramics, and at different ways of putting materials together to make armor that is lighter but just as protective.

Materials engineers can find the best materials to use in many products, from body armor to helicopters.

Hands on

Once the engineers have an idea that they think has a good chance of success, they will use it to create a detailed blueprint or design. This will be used for the next stage of the engineering design process: building a working model or prototype.

A materials engineer may not be involved in the actual design of the product. Rather than work on the **aerodynamics** of a helicopter's body shape, for example, the materials engineer might be researching materials that would reduce **friction** without compromising strength, or develop a new coating for the helicopter body. In designing a new material for use in the helicopter body, the materials engineers might test smaller samples of the material to see if it truly does generate lower friction than the existing material on a helicopter. There may be trade-offs to consider. The coating might add weight to the overall helicopter, and the engineering team would have to decide whether any reduction in friction is worth the added weight.

PROTOTYPES

Every engineer knows that an idea that looks good on paper could still fail when it is tried out in a real situation. The only way to find out if something actually works is to carry out practical tests.

A researcher is shown carrying out tests on protective gloves made from different materials.

Working models: While other engineers build prototypes, the materials engineer is interested in testing samples of possible materials that might be used, perhaps for strength or **durability**. He or she will try to improve the material being tested, perhaps by combining it with other materials or by removing impurities. The material being tested may be rejected altogether, and another material will be pursued.

If the properties of a material are promising, the next step is to test how well it will work in a prototype of the product. This allows the material to be tested under conditions as close as possible to those it will face in actual use. At this stage, the product engineers want to know if the product itself will actually work. For initial testing of the prototype, the materials engineers can suggest possible inexpensive materials to use that will still give realistic results. At the same time, they will continue to research and develop materials that will ensure the finished product works as well as possible.

Back to the drawing board

It is not uncommon for a prototype to fail. Most engineers would be very surprised if their first attempt were entirely successful! They look at the failure of a prototype as a chance to learn and improve their design. The engineers will look very carefully at the flaws in the prototype that caused it to fail. They will take what they have learned and "go back to the drawing board" to start looking for ways they could improve their design.

The engineers will go on looking for ways to improve their original concept until they are as certain as they can be that the idea works and the materials they have chosen to use are the best ones for the project. Only then will the product go into production.

A NEW MATERIAL FOR A BETTER SKATE

Four materials engineering students at the University of Alberta, Canada, won an award for their work in designing a new ice skate that would give better protection to hockey players' feet. They consulted a surgeon to determine which parts of the foot it was most important to protect. The skate was made of **fiberglass** and a mix of polycarbonates—a type of plastic—for a lightweight design. It also had a foam layer inside the skate to make it more comfortable. The students carried out a weight-drop test on their prototype to determine the effects of an impact. They added the fiberglass when they discovered that the skate exploded on impact with the polycarbonate. "It was four months of a lot of work," Dylan Steer, one of the students, said. "Considering we had no budget, it's a decent prototype."

Well-designed skates can protect a player's foot when a skate is used to stop the puck from a powerful slapshot.

TESTING TIMES

Just as a mechanical engineer would test a prototype of a new car engine before putting it in a car, a materials engineer will run tests on samples of materials to see if they perform as hoped.

Computer modeling: In the early stages of the design process, the engineers may try out ideas by running them as computer programs. This is called computer modeling because the model being tested only exists in the computer. It allows engineers to see what might happen to the material if, for example, it is exposed to high temperature or pressure, without having to use up their supplies of what might be an expensive new material.

Materials scientists and engineers at the University of Oxford, England, are developing new super-strong ceramics, which could be used for protective clothing and armored vehicles. They have been using computer models to test how materials react at the microscopic level when they are struck by something else. By understanding how materials react to collisions, the researchers are helping develop new materials that will have a number of valuable uses. Aerospace engineers are using their research to develop new ways to minimize the damage of bird strikes to aircraft, and car manufacturers are making use of their findings to make safer vehicles.

A computer model can show where the weaknesses might be in a component, such as this landing gear for a plane.

Testing to failure

Materials engineers often deliberately push their materials to extremes, until they are destroyed. This is called testing to failure. It tells the engineer what the margin of safety is for the material. This is how much stress the material can withstand before it fails. Knowing this helps to ensure that any product making use of this material can be used safely. It is much better that a concrete block cracks under pressure in a carefully controlled engineering laboratory test than to have it happen unexpectedly when it is used in a bridge somewhere.

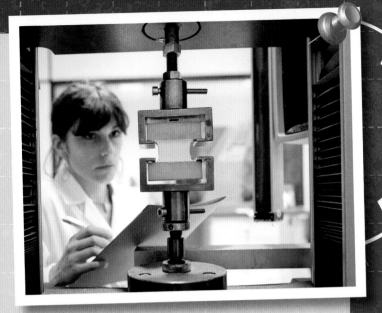

This engineer is testing to see how far a material can be stretched before it breaks.

It is often too expensive to construct an entire object just to destroy it, so the engineers often only test a sample of the material to be used. Once they have done this, they can feed their test results back into their computer models to determine the forces the materials can withstand on a larger scale.

Engineers prepare to test how much heat passes through a material to be used for insulation.

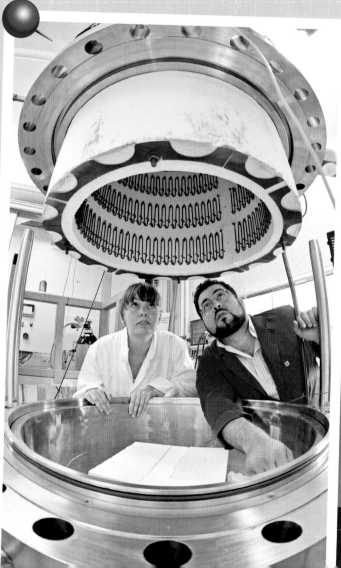

IDEAS INTO PRACTICE

The next stage of the process again involves engineers from different disciplines working together, and sharing the solutions they have found to make a product that works as well as they can make it. The materials engineers will have done their best to come up with an ideal material. It may be just one component used by a sports engineer designing hockey equipment, a chemical engineer designing a waste reclamation plant, an aerospace engineer designing a new aircraft, or a biomedical engineer making a replacement hip.

Putting it all together: There are few things that are made out of just a single material. A car is made of different metals, such as steel, copper, and aluminum, all of which will have been tested by materials engineers specializing in metallurgy. Plastics will be used for some of the lights and fittings, and fabrics for the seat, roof, and floor covers. These will also have needed the expertise of materials engineers. A replacement hip is made from metal, ceramics, and plastic, and all of the materials have to do their job and work together. Materials engineers know the failure of one material affects the performance of the whole product, no matter how good the other materials are.

A successful car design makes use of the specialized knowledge of materials engineers.

Room for improvement: Most of us have probably flown in an aircraft at some point. But one thing you've probably never thought about is that the heat generated by an aircraft engine is so high that the metals in the engine are actually working above their own **melting points**. The reason they don't melt is because many little tubes and holes allow air to cool the engine parts from the inside. The downside is that this airflow slows the plane down. Materials engineers are looking for new solutions to solve this, such as new metal **alloys** with higher melting points or sprayed-on coatings that will raise the melting point so speed won't be affected.

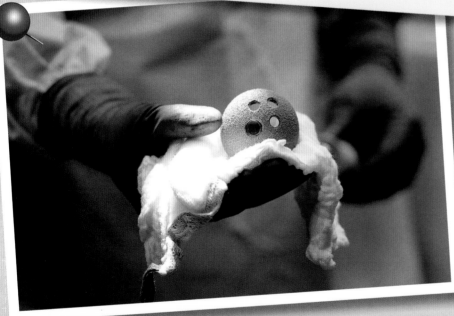

Titanium metal is used in hip replacement components, like this one, because it is strong, lightweight, and doesn't react with body fluids.

FORENSIC ENGINEERING

Materials engineers are often called in to work as forensic engineers. In this capacity, the materials engineers investigate materials that fail or do not work as intended. This could range from something as simple as a toaster that doesn't work properly to the much more serious business of an aircraft crash. The engineers have to collect as much data as they can on the materials that were used, conduct tests and carry out experiments to find out why they failed, and make recommendations for strengthening the materials to avoid future failures.

DESIGN CHALLENGE

Sometimes a material doesn't work perfectly for a given purpose. Combining two or more materials into a new composite can help. As a materials engineer, what can you combine with card stock to create a strong, flexible, lightweight composite?

Materials needed
- Card stock: 10 index cards; approx.
  3 x 5 in (7 x 13 cm)

- Masking tape

- a grapefruit (or similar item)

The following are suggestions:
- Wood: craft sticks,
  toothpicks

- Plastic: straws

- Wire: twist ties,
  unbent paper clips

- Aluminum foil

- Metal: pennies or washers

- Sewing needle, thread

- Glue

1: Define the problem: The card stock represents a new material for high-performance bicycle frames. Roll one index card into a 1-inch (2.5 cm) wide and 6-inch (15 cm) long tube, using one strip of tape along the entire seam. The card is promising because it is lightweight and easily forms tubes. However, it is weak and readily damaged on impact. Your mission: Design, test, and improve a more suitable composite material, combining card stock with other materials.

Hollow tubes made of tough, lightweight, flexible material shaped into tubes could be the basis for parts of a bike frame.

2: Criteria and constraints: Your composite material for a hollow 1 x 6 inch (2.5 x 15 cm) tube should be lightweight, tough, and resist damage on impact. Manufacturers value low cost. That often means a simple design. To keep costs down, add a maximum of three additional materials, preferably fewer, in the smallest amounts possible.

3: Brainstorm: Rev your brain! How could added materials strengthen the card stock? Would you add whole layers or strategically placed pieces? How can you attach them? Think about which card stock properties to retain, and which to enhance. Imagine and sketch several possibilities.

4: Select a solution: Which ideas seem most likely to meet the criteria within the constraints? Zoom in on one idea to develop.

5: Build a prototype: Clarify your idea with a detailed drawing. Plan and show the size, shape, and positions of added materials on the card stock, including any tape or stitches. Make two sets of the same prototype, so you can retest your design. Remember: You are designing only the material, not the tube's structure. When formed, the tube should be hollow.

6: Test the prototype: Does the sheet of material still seem lightweight? Roll it into a 1 x 6 inch (2.5 x 15 cm) tube. Is it flexible enough to be rolled?

Run an impact test. Lay the tube on a counter. Drop the grapefruit on it from 4 inches (10 cm) high. Is the tube damaged? Repeat to check results. Remember: flaws and failures are typical at this stage.

7: Improve the design: What worked well and not so well? Do you need to strengthen the composite or make it more flexible? Can you reduce the amount of additional materials and still get good results? Do you need to make any trade-offs? If you need to make changes, test again.

8: Communicate the solution: Prepare to tell your engineering story. How can you help someone else understand the problem, your process, and the test results? What trade-offs did you make along the way? Using sketches and records, present your story to a family member or friend. Can he or she follow your design drawing to reproduce the material? Answer questions and ask for suggestions for further improvements.

THE FUTURE OF MATERIALS ENGINEERING

New discoveries are being made all the time as new materials are developed that can be built into new technologies. Our requirements for materials change to meet new challenges, especially as we look for ways to live more **sustainably** and make better use of our natural resources.

Things are different at the **nanoscale**. Many materials show unusual properties, such as a very low resistance to electricity or lower melting points. Chemical reactions happen much more quickly at this level, too. The exciting thing is that engineers can begin to plan new devices and applications that can only be made with nanotechnology. Materials scientists and engineers at the Massachusetts Institute of Technology used nanotechnological methods to study the structure of fish scales to help develop more effective ways of designing body armor. The possibilities for nanotech also include computers that are much smaller and faster, super-efficient **solar cells**, and drug treatments that directly target diseased body cells.

A researcher examines nanofibers that might be used to develop new fabrics.

> **Nanotechnology:**
> Nanotechnology deals with the science and engineering of manipulating matter on the level of atoms and molecules. The name comes from the nanometer, a length equal to 1,000 millionth of a meter. To give you an idea of how small that is, a human hair is about 80-100,000 nanometers across.

Working on the nanoscale takes many skills. Biologists, chemists, physicists, and engineers are all involved in exploring this world of the incredibly small. Of particular interest to scientists and engineers are nanotubes. These are made from tightly rolled sheets of carbon, which is a non-metal element, that are just a single atom thick. If the atoms are arranged in the right way, a material can be formed that is six times lighter than steel but hundreds of times stronger.

Origami engineering

Origami is the Japanese art of paperfolding. Today, engineers are being inspired by origami to design materials that are dynamic enough to be useful in structures that bend, stretch, and curve. One everyday example of this is the highly folded and compacted airbag safety feature in cars. Engineers are also experimenting with active materials called magneto-active elastomers. These have the ability to curve and rotate when a **magnetic field** is applied. An elastomer is simply a material that can recover its original shape after being bent and stretched. Solar panels could be built that unfurl like the petals on a flower when the sun shines, then fold themselves away neatly again at night.

This prototype of a solar panel uses magneto-active elastomers.

BIOPLASTICS

Researchers at the University of Georgia are developing bioplastics, which are plastics made from materials harvested from living organisms. One of these is made from albumin, which is found in egg whites. Their aim is to find ways to reduce the amount of petroleum, which will one day run out, used in plastic production and also to make a plastic that is fully biodegradable. They also discovered that the plastics made from albumin had strong antibiotic properties. This means that they could be used for food packaging and in the medical field for things such as wound dressings.

LEARNING MORE

BOOKS

Cook, Eric. *Prototyping* (Makers as Innovators). Cherry Lake Publishing, 2015.

Ebner, Ph.D., Aviva. *Engineering Science Experiments* (Experiments for Future Scientists). Chelsea House, 2011.

Hicks, Kelli. *Analyze This: Testing Materials* (My Science Library). Rourke Publishing Group, 2012.

Larson, Karen. *Changing Matter*. Teacher Created Materials, 2015.

Law, Felicia. *Materials* (Stone Age Science). Crabtree Publishing Co., 2015.

Riley, Peter. *Materials and Properties* (Straight Forward with Science). Franklin Watts, 2015.

ONLINE

www.engineeryourlife.org
A guide to careers in engineering, particularly aimed at girls.

www.science-sparks.com/category/key-stage-2/materials-and-their-properties-key-stage-2
A number of fun experiments exploring the properties of materials.

www.2025labs.com/materials
Introducing materials and their properties.

www.sciencebuddies.org/science-engineering-careers/engineering/materials-scientist-and-engineer
What do materials scientists and engineers do?

PLACES TO VISIT

Museum of Science and Industry, Chicago, Illinois
www.msichicago.org
One of the world's largest science museums with much to discover about materials science and engineering.

GLOSSARY

aerodynamic having a shape that reduces friction when moving through the air

alloy a material made by combining two or more different metals, or a metal and another material

atoms tiny particles from which all materials are made; an atom is the smallest part of an element that can exist

carbon fiber a material made primarily of carbon atoms in a thin, ribbon-like arrangement, generally used as a strengthening material in ceramics and other materials

ceramics materials made from clay that has been hardened by exposure to heat

chemicals substances that often join together and mix with other substances; all of the elements and compounds that make up the materials around us are chemicals

chemical reaction the change that takes place when two or more chemicals react together to form new substances

civil engineer someone responsible for construction and maintenance of structures such as roads, bridges, and buildings

composite material a material made from two or more different materials that each have different properties, such as steel reinforced with carbon fibers

concept map a diagram where related ideas, or concepts, are linked together using arrows

durability the ability to withstand wear and tear

element a substance composed of atoms that cannot be broken down chemically into simpler substances

fiberglass a material made up of very fine fibers of glass

friction one surface, or object, rubbing against another

innovator a person who introduces new ideas, methods, or products

insulators substances that do not readily conduct electricity or heat

limpet a sea creature with a shell that clings tightly to rocks with its feet

lubricant a substance that reduces friction between any two objects, including machine parts, that move in contact with each other

magnetic field the region around a magnet within which the force of magnetism is felt

matter a substance or material that has mass and occupies space

melting point the temperature at which a solid will melt and become liquid

molecule the smallest particle of a substance, consisting of two or more atoms

nanoscale relating to the scale of nanometers —objects that measure between 1 and 100 nanometers long (a thousand millionth to a ten millionth of a meter)

ores rocks from which metals can be obtained

porous able to allow liquid or air to pass through it

properties the characteristics of a material, such as its melting point or ability to stretch

raw materials materials in their natural state from which usable materials are manufactured or extracted

resin a material used as the basis for making plastics, adhesives, and other products

smelt to extract a metal from its rock ore by heating

solar cell a device that converts the light from the Sun into electricity

soluble able to be dissolved

submersible an underwater craft designed for exploration in the deep ocean

sustainably making use of materials in such a way that they will not be used up or wasted

synthetic an artificial material that has been made to imitate a natural material through chemical processes

trade off set aside one criterion so that another more important criterion is met (or prioritized)

INDEX